A CRYPTOZOOLOGIST'S GUIDE TO CURIOUS CREATURES

ANANSI the Talking Spider

AND OTHER LEGENDARY CREATURES OF AFRICA

BY CRAIG BOUTLAND

Gareth Stevens PUBLISHING

Please visit our website, www.garethstevens.com.
For a free color catalog of all our high-quality books,
call toll-free 1-800-542-2595 or fax 1-877-542-2596.

Cataloging-in-Publication Data

Names: Boutland, Craig.
Title: Anansi the talking spider and other legendary creatures of Africa / Craig Boutland.
Description: New York : Gareth Stevens Publishing, 2019. | Series: A cryptozoologist's guide to curious creatures | Includes glossary and index.
Identifiers: LCCN ISBN 9781538227077 (pbk.) | ISBN 9781538227060 (library bound) | ISBN 9781538227084 (6 pack)
Subjects: LCSH: Mythology, African--Juvenile literature. | Animals, Mythical--Juvenile literature. Cryptozoology--Juvenile literature.
Classification: LCC BL2400.B68 2019 | DDC 398.2096--dc23

Published in 2019 by
Gareth Stevens Publishing
111 East 14th Street, Suite 349
New York, NY 10003

For Brown Bear Books Ltd:
Editor: Dawn Titmus
Designer: Lynne Lennon
Editorial Director: Lindsey Lowe
Children's Publisher: Anne O'Daly
Design Manager: Keith Davis
Picture Manager: Sophie Mortimer

Picture credits:
Front Cover: istockphoto
Interior: Abe Books: 16tl; **Amazon:** 23; **Antiquarianauctions.com:** 16tr; **Getty Images:** Ariadne Van Zandbergen, 27, 29; **istockphoto:** 1, fotogaby, 9r; **Public Domain:** Jeff McArthur, 13; **Shutterstock:** 3dMotus, 19, fivespots, 19, Felix Lipov, 14, Pieljoy, 15, reptiles4all, 17, Sergey Uryadnikov, 28, Vladimir Wrangel, 20; **Thinkstock:** istockphoto, 9l, MR1805, 21, Sergeij Petrakov, 10; **Topfoto:** Fortean, 25, The Granger Collection, 11, Ullsteinbild, 26, World History Archive, 6; **Trowicia:** 7; **UFO Centre:** 22.

Key: t=top, b=bottom, c=center, l=left, r=right

Manufactured in the United States of America
1 2 3 4 5 6 7 8 9 12 11 10

CPSIA compliance information: Batch #CS18GS. For further information contact Gareth Stevens, New York, New York at 1-800-542-2595.

CONTENTS

WORDS IN THE GLOSSARY APPEAR IN BOLD TYPE THE FIRST TIME THEY ARE USED IN THE TEXT.

CURIOUS CREATURES

All over the world, there are stories about curious and amazing creatures. These animals often appear in **myths** and **legends**. In Puerto Rico, one story tells of a bloodsucking monster. In Ireland, there are **rumors** about giant snakelike creatures that live in lakes. In Russian **folklore**, there is a tale about a witch who traps children in her forest hut. Do these incredible creatures really exist? Or are they just stories?

Many people think such creatures do exist and say they have seen them. Some even claim they have photos and videos. The search for these creatures and other animals thought to be **extinct** is called cryptozoology. "Crypto" means "hidden," and zoology is the study of animals.

IN THIS BOOK

In Africa, there are many stories about legendary creatures. In this book, we look at the stories about Anansi the spider, the Grootslang cave monster, the Mokele-mbembe dinosaur, and the Nandi Bear. Now read on...

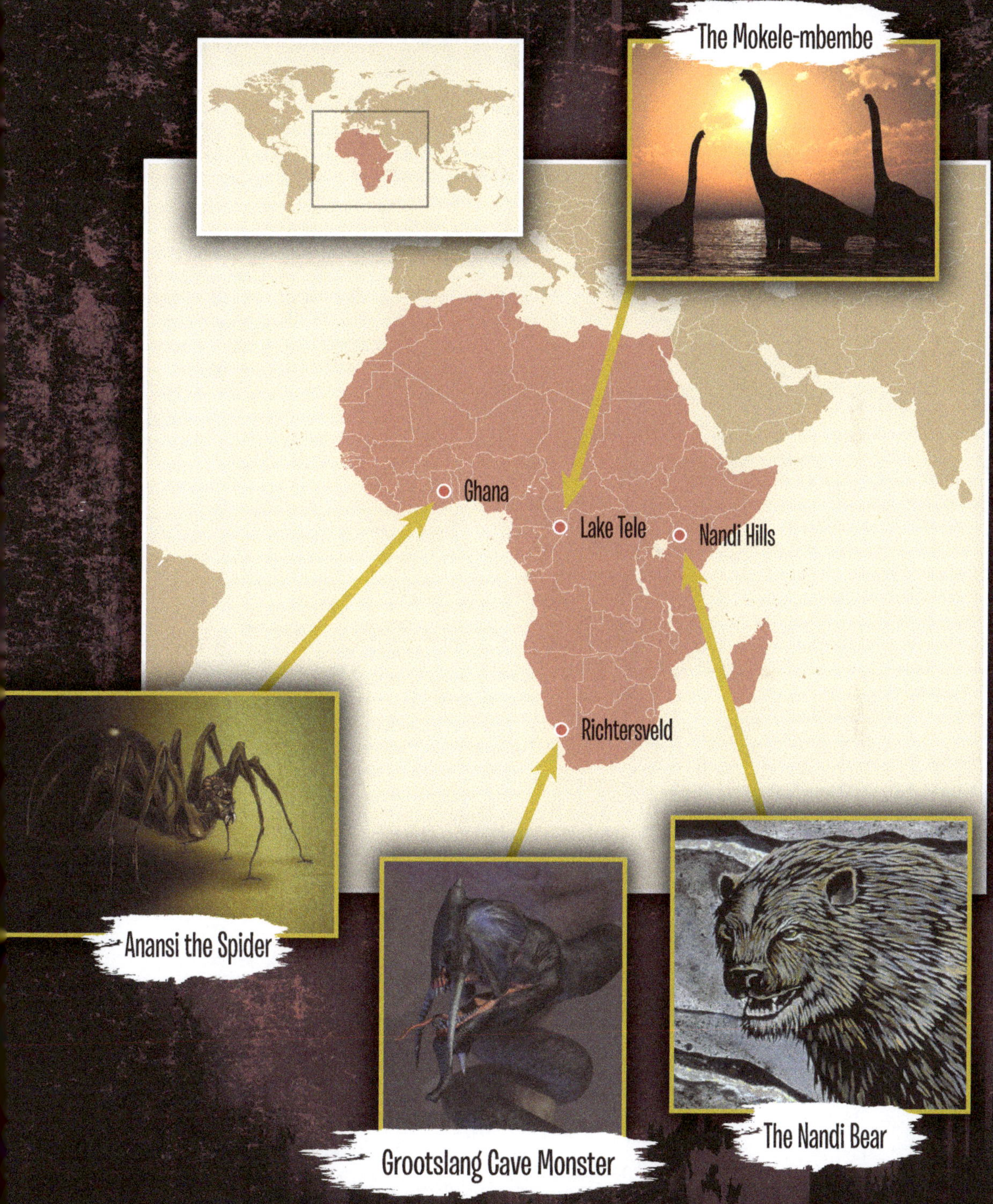
The Mokele-mbembe
Ghana
Lake Tele
Nandi Hills
Richtersveld
Anansi the Spider
Grootslang Cave Monster
The Nandi Bear

ANANSI THE SPIDER

Imagine a giant eight-legged creature that likes to play tricks and cause trouble! This is the description of Anansi the spider, a key character in West African **folktales**. Although not physically strong, Anansi is intelligent, and his cunning allows him to outwit much bigger, stronger animals.

Stories about Anansi originally came from the Akan people, who lived in what is now Ghana. West Africans told many tales about animal tricksters, which are animals that are clever but mischievous. Most tricksters are able to change their appearance to look like humans or other animals. Anansi the spider is the most popular trickster. There are many different stories about him.

A spider and its web decorate this **staff** that was used by high-ranking Akan officials.

An artist's impression of what the mischievous trickster Anansi the Spider might look like!

FACT BEHIND THE LEGEND

There have been many stories of giant spiders in the jungles of Central Africa. They are known by the name J'ba fofi. One report from the mid-1900s said the spider was the size of a small mammal, with a leg span of 5 feet (1.5 m). However, reports of such huge spiders cannot always be taken seriously. The body weight of such creatures could not be supported by regular spider legs. The biggest known spiders are tarantulas, especially the Goliath Birdeater. It has a leg span almost 10 inches (25 cm) wide.

STORYTELLING

One story describes how Anansi gave storytelling to the world. There were no stories in the world because they were all owned by Nyame, the sky god. Nyame said he would release the stories if Anansi brought him Onini the **python**, Osebo the leopard, and a nest of **hornets**—all creatures stronger or more dangerous than Anansi.

Nyame thought Anansi would fail. But Anansi persuaded Onini to let himself be tied to a palm branch so that his length could be measured accurately. Anansi said the python had to be tied to the palm branch so that he was straight. As soon as Onini was tied up, Anansi took him to Nyame.

Next, Anansi dug a hole in the ground. When Osebo fell into the hole, Anansi offered to help him out by spinning webs. The leopard climbed out of the hole, but he was caught in Anansi's webs. Anansi took Osebo to Nyame.

Finally, Anansi tricked the hornets into believing it was raining. He poured water over himself and the hornets' nest from a **calabash**. He said the hornets could stay dry if they sheltered inside the calabash. When they flew into the calabash, Anansi put a stopper in the pot and carried it to Nyame. Anansi had completed all his tasks, and Nyame kept his promise. He gave all the stories of the world to Anansi and made him the god of storytelling.

In one story, Anansi captures Osebo the leopard in his webs and takes Osebo to Nyame.

Anansi tricks a swarm of hornets to shelter in a calabash. Then he traps them inside.

BIRTH OF A LEGEND

In some stories about Anansi, he is selfish, out to make life enjoyable for himself, not for others. The only time Anansi was outwitted was when he came upon the wax model of a girl. He mistook the model for a real person, and when she wouldn't speak to him, he kicked her with one of his legs. His leg stuck to the wax, so to free his leg, he kicked the wax model with another leg. Every time he kicked, another leg got stuck. Finally, all eight of his legs were stuck. Anansi was made to look as foolish as the other animals he had played his tricks on.

The stories of Anansi spread by word of mouth from Ghana to neighboring African countries. In the 1600s, European slave traders kidnapped Africans from their homes and forced them to work on plantations in the Caribbean and the Americas. The slaves brought the folktales of Africa with them. It is possible that trickster tales were popular and spread throughout the world because they gave hope to people who felt powerless in life.

The tale of Anansi and the wax model may have been the basis for one of the most famous folktales in the United States. In 1881, Joel Chandler Harris wrote about Brer (Brother) Rabbit in his first book, *Uncle Remus: His Songs and His Sayings*, which retold the folktales Harris had heard from former slaves in the southern United States. The cunning Brer Fox created a person out of tar, and when Brer Rabbit came across it, he started hitting it because it did not answer him. His feet stuck to the tar, but Brer Rabbit freed himself because he was able to persuade Brer Fox to throw him into a briar patch. From there, he was able to escape. In many ways, the character of Brer Rabbit is a descendant of Anansi, a clever animal that uses his wits to get out of trouble.

This illustration shows Brer Rabbit stuck to tar, while Brer Fox rolls around laughing.

GROOTSLANG
CAVE MONSTER

According to legend, a huge creature lives deep in the caves of the Richtersveld region of South Africa and guards a valuable treasure. When Dutch farmers first **colonized** South Africa in the 1700s, they named the creature Grootslang, or Grote Slang, which means "big snake." Some people believe there is still a giant snake waiting to be discovered.

Thousands of years before the Dutch colonists arrived in South Africa, the Africans told stories about monsters that lurked in the caves. One tale described how, when the gods made the first animals, they made a mistake. They made the first creatures as strong and intelligent as they could, hoping the animals would be perfect. But the gods soon realized that these creatures could be cruel as well as good, so they began to turn them into other creatures, such as elephants and snakes. Although the gods managed to catch and change most of the original creatures, one escaped and made its home in a giant cave, where it multiplied.

The Grootslang is depicted as a terrifying-looking creature that is part elephant and part snake in this artist's impression.

There are similar stories in other parts of Africa, including one from Benin, in West Africa. This describes a monster with an elephant's head and a snake's tail. But most stories about the Grootslang have come from the Richtersveld region, a dry and mountainous area just south of the Orange River in South Africa's Northern Cape province.

THE BOTTOMLESS PIT

The Richtersveld is now a national park on the border with the country of Namibia. There are ancient Nama rock paintings of large serpents in this region, and some of the serpents are shown with horns. The Nama are one of the oldest cultures in southern Africa. Before the arrival of the white colonists, they lived as nomads herding cattle.

A deep limestone cave in the Richtersveld is said to be guarded by the Grootslang.

DIAMOND MINING

South Africa is one of the world's major diamond producers. Diamonds were first discovered on the south bank of the Orange River around 1866. Europeans flocked to South Africa, all eager to make their fortunes. It may be that new colonists used the legend of the Grootslangs to frighten off other settlers. Or perhaps indigenous peoples wanted to protect their homeland from European colonists.

Archaeologists have found evidence that tens of thousands of years ago, people in this region worshiped large snakes, such as the python, as gods.

A deep limestone cave, the Wondergat ("Mystery Hole") or Heitsi Eibib ("emptiness" in the Nama language), lies in the southwest of the Richtersveld. According to local legends, the cavern is full of diamonds said to be guarded by the Grootslang that lives in the cave. Some say there may be underground tunnels linking the cave to the sea. The coast is about 40 miles (65 km) away. However, no proof of the tunnels has ever been found.

Some eyewitnesses say they have seen enormous pythons near the cave. One report said the snake was 50 feet (15 m) long. Could this have been responsible for the disappearance of an English explorer?

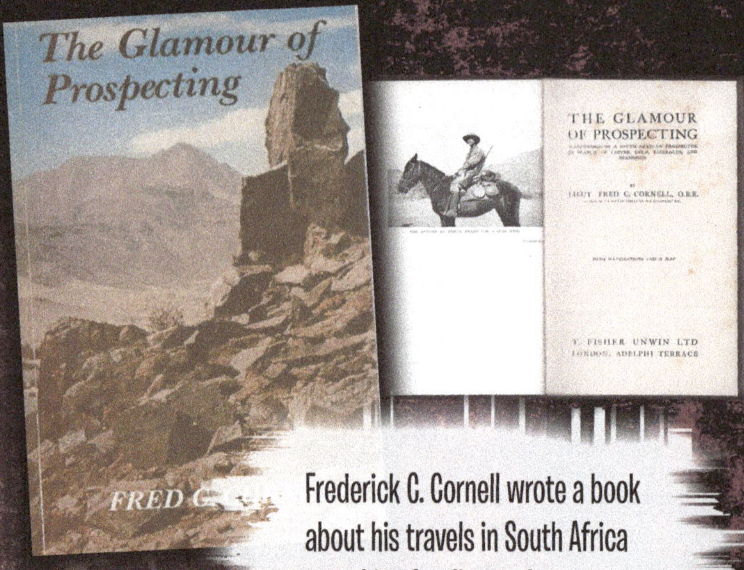

Frederick C. Cornell wrote a book about his travels in South Africa searching for diamonds.

In 1917, Peter Grayson led an **expedition** to the Richtersveld area to look for diamonds. A lion killed one member of the team and injured another. When a couple of the other men fell sick, they abandoned the expedition. But Grayson decided to stay and continue the search. Shortly afterward, he disappeared, and his body was never found. Local people said the Grootslang must have killed him because he had uncovered the store of diamonds it was protecting.

Whether or not they are Grootslang, there have been sightings of giant snakes throughout the area, particularly giant snakes that live in the Orange River. In 1920, another English diamond seeker, Frederick C. Cornell, saw the head and neck of a large snake swimming in the water along the Orange River. He claimed to have fought it and other snakes off by dropping sticks of **dynamite** into the river to keep the snakes from attacking his mules.

The stories about the Grootslang are a strange mix of ancient legend and modern ideas about the value of diamonds—and the need to protect them from thieves! Nevertheless, there may be some truth in the stories of giant snakes living in caves. The Richtersveld is a remote area. There could be something unknown—or at the very least a large python—living in the Mystery Hole, yet to be found.

FACT BEHIND THE LEGEND

It seems likely that the Grootslang is a giant python. The largest python in Africa is the African rock python. The average adult measures about 10 to 16 feet (3 to 5 m), but some can reach 23 feet (7 m) or more. Another possibility is that the creature is a water monitor. This is Africa's largest lizard. Although they like to live close to water, they travel long distances on land looking for food, and they can even climb trees!

The African rock python is feared across Africa. It kills its prey by squeezing it tightly.

THE MOKELE-MBEMBE

Do dinosaurs still roam the earth? Birds are descendants of dinosaurs, but cryptozoologists believe that a giant **sauropod** lives on in the basin of the Congo River in Central Africa. They claim this creature is related to the giants of the dinosaur age—the **brachiosaurus** and **apatosaurus** that walked the earth 150 million years ago.

Lake Tele lies in a remote part of the Republic of the Congo, in a region of swampy forests. The lake is supposedly the home of the Mokele-mbembe—meaning "one who stops the flow of rivers" in the Lingala language. The creature is described as being a large reptilelike beast with a grayish body, long neck, small head, and long tail. Some reports also describe it as having a single horn on its head.

NEW CREATURES

In the early 1900s, European explorers heard many stories of strange creatures from the remote regions of Central Africa. Although many descriptions sounded unbelievable, some turned out to be details of new species that were unknown at the time. A creature that was said to be half giraffe and half zebra turned out to be the **okapi**.

The brachiosaurus was a giant dinosaur that roamed the earth 150 million years ago. Is there a creature like it still in the Congo?

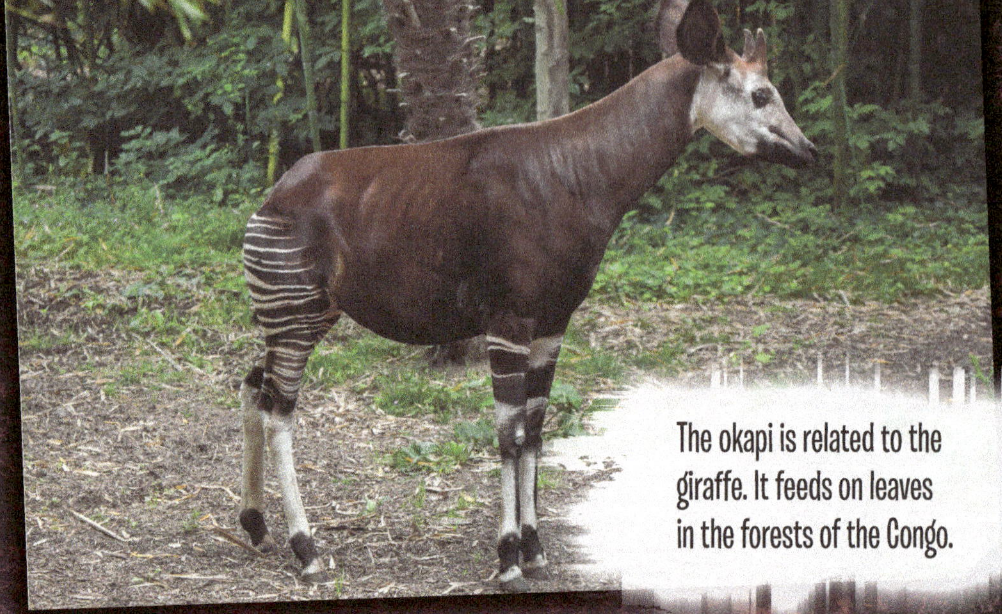

The okapi is related to the giraffe. It feeds on leaves in the forests of the Congo.

The okapi is an animal with a long neck and zebralike stripes on its hindquarters. Such discoveries gave **credibility** to descriptions of other curious creatures.

In 1913, German explorer Captain Freiherr von Stein zu Lausnitz heard descriptions of an "animal said to be of a brownish-gray color with a smooth skin, its size approximately that of an elephant. … It is said to have a long and very flexible neck. … A few spoke about a long flexible tail … its diet is said to be entirely vegetable. The preferred plant was shown to me, it is a kind of **liana** with large white blossoms." Because the creature was a plant eater, von Stein thought it more likely to be an undiscovered animal species, rather than just a myth. His belief was strengthened when he heard the same description of the creature from a number of independent sources.

HOW STRANGE!

The idea that the Mokele-mbembe might be a sauropod dinosaur came about because the description seemed to match the dinosaur skeletons that were found and assembled in Western museums during the early 1900s. However, there have been no findings of such big fossils in Africa. Some zoologists believe that a more likely identity for the Mokele-mbembe is the *Paraceratherium*, an extinct ancestor of the modern rhinoceros. These animals had long necks and were huge. Could a type of long-necked rhinoceros live in the swamps around Lake Tele?

Paraceratherium stood 18 feet (5.5 m) at the shoulder and was much larger than the modern rhino.

Cryptozoologists continued to search for Mokele-mbembe, and reported sightings continued from the 1920s to the 1970s. They all seemed to agree that the animal had three toes, that it was dangerous but did not kill or eat the people or other creatures it attacked, and that its food was the flowering liana plant.

FIRST REAL EVIDENCE?

In 1979, a **missionary** named Eugene Thomas told James Powell and Roy Mackal (two dedicated cryptozoologists) that the local people claimed to have killed and eaten a Mokole-mbembe in about 1960. He said it had wounded itself on a spiked fence the indigenous peoples had built to stop it interfering with their fishing in the north end of Lake Tele. Those who had eaten the Mokole-mbembe later died. It was described as reddish-brown and larger than an elephant, with a long neck, a frill on a small, snakelike head, and four thick, short legs with claws.

French cryptozoologist Michel Ballot found huge footprints in his search for the Mokole-mbembe.

Roy Mackal wrote a book about his two expeditions searching for the Mokele-mbembe.

Mackal was fascinated. In the 1960s, he had searched the waters of Loch Ness in Scotland for the similarly **elusive** Loch Ness Monster. After hearing about Mokele-mbembe, he set out on an expedition in 1980 to see if he could find it. He had no luck, but the following year, he tried again. Once again, he failed, but the many descriptions he heard—of animals 15 to 30 feet (4.5 to 9 m) long, with snakelike heads and necks and long, thin tails—led him to believe there must be something out there in the jungle swamps.

By 2011, there had been some 50 expeditions to find Mokele-mbembe, but evidence was just one fuzzy photo and a few footprints. Some local people around Lake Tele think of Mokele-mbembe as a spiritual being, rather than a physical beast, but still believe it exists. Mackal also agrees that something exists: "I'm interested in discovering unknown species of animals. . . . But I think Mokele-mbembe still exist, and there isn't just one—they are reproducing."

THE NANDI BEAR

For centuries, the Nandi people of western Kenya, in East Africa, have told tales of a ferocious animal that roams the Nandi Hills at night, killing people and livestock and eating their brains. The creature is named the Nandi Bear for the Nandi, although in the language of the people, it is called the "*kerit.*"

To the Nandi people and other indigenous peoples in East Africa, the Nandi Bear is a mythical beast, almost an evil spirit. The head of a Nandi village described the creature as being: "a devil which prowls the *nganasa* [hut settlement] on the darkest nights, seeking people, especially children, to devour; it is half like a man and half like a huge, ape-faced bird, and you may know it at once from its fearful howling roar, and because in the dark of night its mouth glows red like the embers of a log."

EUROPEAN COLONIZATION

In the early 1900s, European colonists also gave detailed descriptions of the creature. These accounts, combined with the Nandi people's stories, lead some cryptozoologists to believe the Nandi Bear is real. They think it is a creature that has survived undetected for thousands of years.

This illustration of the Nandi Bear shows it looking like a giant hyena with a bearlike head.

Two European settlers are pictured here with East Africans in a village in the early 1900s.

European colonists who saw the creature all agree that it looked like a bear and walked like a bear, although it was also often described as being like a large hyena. Its height was said to be between 4 and 6 feet (1.2 and 1.8 m) at rear and front legs, and it was described as having a sloping back and large jaws. Its color was said to be brownish red to dark brown, and some people also claimed the animal was able to climb trees.

EYEWITNESSES AGREE

In 1912, a settler named Major Toulson was called to see a "leopard" that was prowling near his farm. He reported: "I rushed out at once and saw a strange beast making off: it appeared to have long hair behind and was rather low in front … it appeared to be black, with a gait [walk] similar to that of a bear—a kind of shuffling walk."

Other witnesses agreed that it was not a hyena, but said it was something very like a bear. Geoffrey Williams described what he saw while he was camping in Uasin Gishu county in Kenya: "In size it was, I should say, larger than the bear that lives in the pit at the 'Zoo' and it was quite as heavily built. The fore quarters were very thickly furred, as were all four legs, but the hindquarters were comparatively speaking smooth or bare … the head was long and pointed and exactly like that of a bear."

The Nandi Bear is said to roam the land around the Nandi Hills at night, seeking prey to kill.

HOW STRANGE!

The only native bear known to have lived in Africa in modern times is the Atlas bear. It was thought to have been hunted to extinction in the late 1800s. Atlas bears had dark brownish-black fur on their backs and a brighter reddish fur on their undersides. But unlike descriptions of the Nandi Bear, they were not good tree climbers. And they were seen only in North Africa, in the Atlas Mountains. It would have been difficult if not impossible for them to have crossed the Sahara Desert and moved south into Kenya. If Nandi was a bear, it is most likely, perhaps, to have been the common European brown bear, which somehow found its way south to East Africa.

The brown bear lives in northern areas of North America, Europe, and Asia. Is it possible one moved as far south as East Africa?

FURTHER INFORMATION

Books

Arnosky, Jim.
Monster Hunt: Exploring Mysterious Creatures. New York, NY: Disney-Hyperion, 2011.

Gerhard, Ken.
A Menagerie of Mysterious Beasts: Encounters with Cryptid Creatures. Woodbury, MN: Llewellyn Worldwide, 2016.

Halls, Kelly Milner, Rick Spears, and Roxyanne Young.
Tales of the Cryptids: Mysterious Creatures That May or May Not Exist. Minneapolis, MN: Lerner Publishing Group, 2006.

Websites

anansistories.com
Page with links to stories about Anansi the spider.

wiki.kidzsearch.com/wiki/Cryptozoology
A page for kids about cryptozoology, with links to creatures.

www.newanimal.org
A website on cryptozoology, with links to pages on creatures.

INDEX